BIG-TIME BUSINESS

SKIN DEEP
THE BUSINESS OF BEAUTY

Angela Royston

W
FRANKLIN WATTS
LONDON • SYDNEY

Franklin Watts
First published in Great Britain in 2015 by The Watts Publishing Group

Produced by Calcium

Acknowledgements:
The publisher would like to thank the following for permission to reproduce photographs: Cover: Shutterstock: Kayros Studio l, Aleksandr Markin r. Inside: Dreamstime: Goodscents 19br, Jperagine 31t; Istockphoto: Ariwasabi 3cr, Joel Carillet 11t, Diego Cervo 41t, Duncan1890 7, Ann Marie Kurtz 40bl, Catherine Lane 8cl, Kristian Sekulic 10cl; Shutterstock: Africa Studio 24, AISPIX by Image Source 30–31c, 34tr, 39c, Altafulla 5tc, Anna Baburkina 35t, Dean Bertoncelj 29t, Stefano Cavoretto 13, Diego Cervo 32tr, Claires 1br, Conrado 27t, Creatista 42b, Phil Date 38r, Dainis Derics 20b, Zhu Difeng 9t, Helga Esteb 36bl, 44bl, Featureflash 45, Richard Griffin 5br, Goodluz 18, CandyBox Images 33b, Raisa Kanareva 37tr, Mangostock 21, Stuart Miles 15tr, Felix Mizioznikov 28cl, Luba V Nel 1bl, Vasilchenko Nikita 17r, Monika Olszewska 14–15c, Edyta Pawlowska 43, Andrey Popov 23cl, Dooley Productions 26br, Gina Smith 16b, SVLuma 13br, Syda Productions 12, Szefei 22br, Liviu Toader 13bl, Vladimir Wrangel 6br, NataliaYeromina 4–5c, Dusan Zidar 25tr.

Dewey number 338.4'76467
ISBN 978 1 4451 3921 0

Printed in China

Franklin Watts
An imprint of
Hachette Children's Group
Part of The Watts Publishing Group
Carmelite House
50 Victoria Embankment
London EC4Y 0DZ

An Hachette UK Company
www.hachette.co.uk

www.franklinwatts.co.uk

CONTENTS

FACING THE FUTURE

Do you see pound signs when you look at your face? The cosmetic industry does! Every year, billions of pounds are spent on products that promise to make us look and feel great. So, who are the big beauty buyers of the future and how is the industry cashing in on their obsession with good looks?

Forever young

In 2005, the average age girls began to use beauty products was 17. Today, it is just 11, and girls as young as six are already wearing cosmetics! The industry hopes that by hooking these youthful cosmetic fans now, they will buy into beauty for the rest of their lives.

Every day, we are bombarded with images of gorgeous celebrities, models and actresses. The pressure to look good has never been so intense.

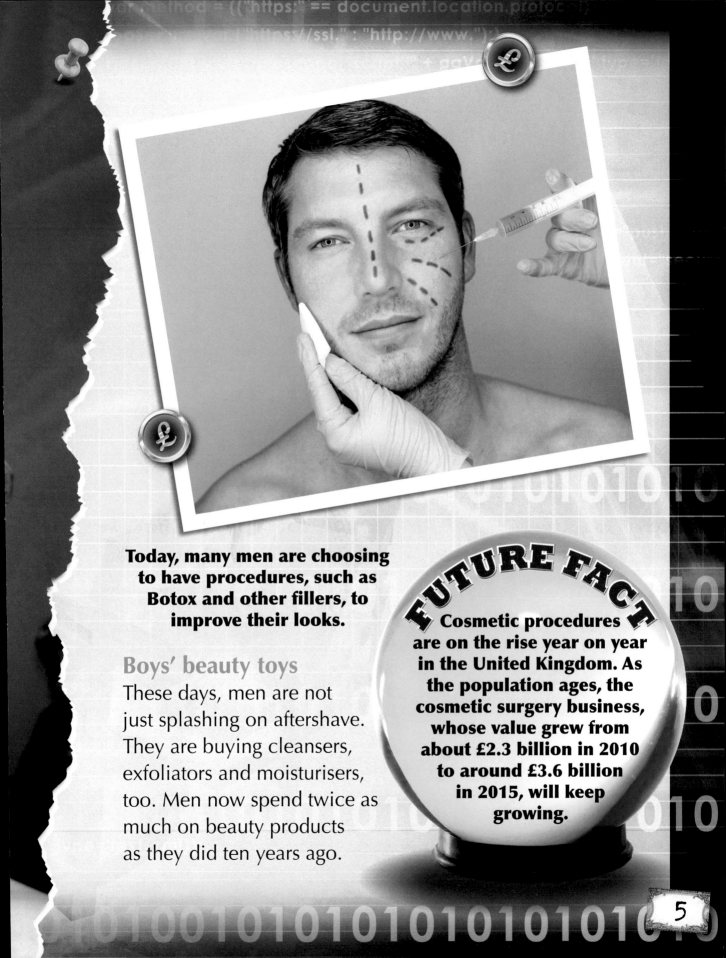

Today, many men are choosing to have procedures, such as Botox and other fillers, to improve their looks.

Boys' beauty toys

These days, men are not just splashing on aftershave. They are buying cleansers, exfoliators and moisturisers, too. Men now spend twice as much on beauty products as they did ten years ago.

FUTURE FACT

Cosmetic procedures are on the rise year on year in the United Kingdom. As the population ages, the cosmetic surgery business, whose value grew from about £2.3 billion in 2010 to around £3.6 billion in 2015, will keep growing.

A LONG HISTORY

Is beauty a modern craze? Certainly people are using more cosmetics today than ever before, but the idea of beauty is thousands of years old. Women in ancient Egypt used black kohl to outline their eyes and that was 6,000 years ago!

Rich and beautiful

In the past, cosmetics were used mainly by rich people and by entertainers. In the sixteenth century, Queen Elizabeth I of England painted her face white to cover up smallpox scars and, as she grew older, she dyed her hair red. In the eighteenth century, fashionable men and women powdered their faces and wore wigs.

This bust of Queen Nefertiti of ancient Egypt shows her wearing kohl around her eyes.

Look like a film star

Cosmetics became cheaper and more popular in the 1920s and 1930s. Women copied the look of film stars, such as Greta Garbo. The Max Factor company supplied cosmetics for the stars of the screen and soon for ordinary people, too.

Queen Elizabeth I of England used cosmetics to make herself look younger and more beautiful.

THE INDUSTRY TODAY

How did the industry grow so big? After the Second World War (1939–45), the lives of people in Europe, the United States and other richer regions changed dramatically. With peace came greater wealth and more spending money. Sales of fridges, televisions and other appliances rocketed, as did sales of cosmetics.

The giants

The United States leads the way in the cosmetics industry. Of the 100 biggest companies, nearly one-third are American, and their earnings have grown fast. For example, in 1983, Estée Lauder sold cosmetics worth £600 million in total. By 2013, just 30 years later, its sales had risen to £6 billion.

Estée Lauder products are some of the most widely sold cosmetics in the world.

About £35 billion is spent on cosmetics each year in Asia and Australia alone.

FUTURE FACT

At present, the countries that supply and buy the most cosmetics are the United States, France, Japan and Brazil, but the markets in China, India and other countries are growing fast.

Thousands of jobs

Many people are employed by the world's big beauty companies, in research, factories, advertising and sales. Many of the products created are bought by hairdressers, beauty therapists, manicurists and other people with specialised skills. These people are employed in thousands of small businesses.

WHO'S BEHIND THE PRODUCT?

Where does the shampoo you use come from?

The simple answer is the shop where you bought it, but a lot happens to shampoo and all beauty products before they reach the shelf. Beauty companies stay in business by producing a constant supply of new or improved products. In 2013, L'Oréal registered 624 new products!

Creating the product

Cosmetic chemists are scientists who experiment with ingredients and design new products. They find the best mixture of ingredients to give a particular result. The chemists then test the products to make sure they work and are safe.

A cosmetic chemist tests various chemicals to get the effect she wants, including the exact colour and smell.

Many cosmetics companies are choosing celebrities, such as Eva Longoria, to promote their products.

Advertising and selling

Once the product is ready to launch, the advertising and sales departments go into action. They want customers to buy all their products – the existing ones as well as the new ones. Adverts on television, in magazines and on posters catch your eye, but sales people have to get the new products into the shops and salons.

FUTURE FACT

Cosmetics companies advertise and sell their products online, as well as through the usual channels, such as shops and salons. In 2010, online sales were only 4 per cent of the cosmetics industry's total sales, but this will increase rapidly.

LOOKING GOOD

Who buys beauty products?

You might think the answer to this is 'women', but men, too, want to look their best. Looking good makes people feel more confident. The beauty industry makes billions of pounds every year helping people to look as attractive as possible.

Everyone wants to look their best when they are in a photo with their friends.

Increasing demand

Cosmetics companies help to create the desire for beauty products. They encourage us to admire glamorous film stars, models and other celebrities, and want us to think that using the same cosmetics as the stars will make us more beautiful, too.

Businesses making billions

Beauty companies, such as L'Oréal, sell billions of pounds' worth of cosmetics every year and the amount is growing. In 2008, L'Oréal sold cosmetics worth £14 billion. By 2013, sales had increased to £18 billion.

Many young men examine themselves in the mirror just as much as young women do.

WHAT THE WORLD SPENDS

In 2010, economists estimated that people spent £99 billion on cosmetics. About 27 per cent was spent on skincare, 20 per cent on haircare, 20 per cent on make-up and 33 per cent on products such as sunscreens.

CHAPTER 2
MAKE-UP MAGIC

What does make-up do? Make-up can subtly change the way a face looks. If skin is too pale, blusher will add colour. Make-up for eyes is designed to make eyes look bigger. Pale lipstick can make lips look fuller and bright lipstick can create a dramatic look.

Variety of products

Each brand of cosmetics has a huge range of products, including dozens of colours of lipstick, eyeshadow and nail polish, as well as skincare products. Each big company owns several different brands. So one company will produce and sell hundreds of different products.

14

Eye make-up includes eyeshadow, eye liner, mascara and eyebrow pencil.

A mascara wand curls the eyelashes and applies mascara to make the eyelashes look thicker.

FUTURE FACT

Men are beginning to buy make-up, such as concealer to cover spots and skin blemishes and clear mascara for their eyelashes. The market is still small, but it is likely to become bigger in the future.

Selling technique

Companies that sell expensive brands, such as Lancôme or Chanel, train their sales teams to also 'cross sell'. A customer who goes into a store to buy lipstick, for example, will be encouraged to buy lip liner and lip gloss, too.

MAKE-OVER

What's a make-over all about? A make-over is when a trained beauty therapist selects products from a company's range and uses them to make up a customer. The customer has make-up applied by an expert, and the company sells products.

In some stores, a beauty therapist will give a free make-over, but in most cases the make-over has to be booked and paid for.

Promoting new products

There are so many make-up products to choose from, but many customers go on buying just their usual ones. In a make-over, the beauty therapist will discuss all the products with the customer and choose the ones that suit her best. This introduces the customer to new products.

Make-up is designed to compliment a person's skin tone, however light or dark.

Free samples

Giving away free samples is another way of tempting people to try the latest cosmetics. Once the customer has tried the sample, the company hopes that he or she will buy the product. Also, some people are tempted into buying an expensive product because it comes with some free samples.

LOOKING AFTER SKIN

How many different creams and lotions do you rub into your skin? The answer for most people is quite a few. Skincare is big business, partly because almost everyone uses skincare products, including men of all ages and children.

Even older men are using skincare products to help fight the effects of ageing.

Clean and moist

From the moment you step under the shower, you are giving money to the cosmetics industry. You almost certainly use shower gel or soap, possibly followed by various lotions. Even babies have their own range of products, from baby wipes to creams and oils. By 2017, the global baby-care market is expected to reach £39 billion.

Natural or organic?

The cosmetics industry uses both 'natural' and 'organic' to describe chemical-free ingredients. Sales of skincare products that use these ingredients are growing. Between 2012 and 2013, sales of organic health and beauty products in the United Kingdom grew by 17 per cent to £37.2 million. This is set to increase even more in the future.

Beauty companies are finding that products that carry a 'no animal testing' label are selling well.

ANIMAL TESTING

Many groups around the world oppose the testing of cosmetics on animals. These groups say that animal testing is not only cruel, but also unnecessary. In March 2103, the European Union banned the testing of cosmetics on animals. The practice, however, continues in some countries, including the United States.

NO ANIMAL TESTING
CRUELTY FREE
NO ANIMAL TESTING

DARKER OR LIGHTER?

What is the best colour for skin?

There is, of course, no 'best' colour, but that does not stop people spending money trying to make their skin darker or lighter. However, doctors warn that by doing so, many people are putting their health at risk.

Some people claim that using a tanning lamp or tanning bed is safer than sunbathing, because you can control the amount of radiation that hits your skin.

Getting a tan

Many people want a suntan. Sunscreens help to protect against the damaging effects of the sun's rays, but around 10 per cent of people in the United Kingdom never use sunscreen. The discovery of a link between sunbeds and skin cancer has meant a drop in the number of tanning salons. This has led, though, to a big growth in the fake-tan business – now worth more than £100 million a year and one of the fastest-growing sectors in the cosmetics industry.

The sale of suncare products is fairly constant, although it increases in particularly hot summers.

Lighten up

Skin lighteners are used to get rid of dark marks or acne scars, as well as to lighten skin. It is estimated that women in Asia spend £10 billion a year on skin lighteners. Many lighteners, however, contain chemicals that can cause allergic reactions or skin cancer.

RED ALERT

Tanning beds are dangerous. The risk of someone who uses them getting skin cancer doubles after just seven sessions, and the younger the person is, the more dangerous it is. In the United Kingdom, the use of tanning beds has been banned for anyone younger than 18.

21

BEAUTY TREATMENTS

A massage makes the skin healthy and glowing. It relaxes the muscles under the skin and so helps to soften frown lines.

Beauty treatments are big business. Most women in the United Kingdom spend over £1,000 a year on beauty treatments, which can include facials, manicures for hands and pedicures for feet. And that's only part of what a beauty salon or spa might offer. Customers can also relax in steam rooms and pools or indulge in aromatherapy or meditation.

Lie back and relax

People may simply go to a spa to relax or to give their body an intense workout. This can include deep cleaning and moisturising of the skin, hair removal, body scrubs and massages of the whole body or just the head, shoulders or neck.

Treating yourself

A trip to a spa can be expensive, but more and more people are prepared to pay for the treat. In the United Kingdom, over £5 billion is spent each year in more than 800 spas. Worldwide, the spa business is worth £40 billion.

Painting toenails is part of a pedicure.

FUTURE FACT

According to the Australian government, in 2012 there were nearly 100,000 people working in the hair and beauty industries in Australia. That number is expected to increase by more than 5 per cent each year up to 2017.

CHAPTER 3

ALL ABOUT HAIR

A new hairstyle is an easy way to look different. Hair is so important to the way we look that people spend more on hair products than on make-up. In 2014, people around the world spent more than £50 billion on hair products, which could rise to nearly £59 billion by 2020.

Shampoos, gels, conditioners, dyes, mousses, oils... there are hundreds of different hair products. Sales dropped off during the global economic recession that began in 2008 but have been rising every year since 2012.

Caring for hair

Haircare is big business. In 2013, people in the United Kingdom spent £1.7 billion on haircare products – that's more than 20 per cent of all cosmetics and over £45 for each person. The biggest companies include Estée Lauder, L'Oréal and Proctor & Gamble. Each company makes a wide range of products that suit every type of hair.

Many men use hair gel or wax to keep their style in place.

FUTURE FACT

Shampoos and conditioners that are made with organic ingredients cost more to buy, yet their sales are increasing faster than most beauty products. All the big companies have natural and organic brands, and some companies produce nothing else.

Growing haircare

Haircare products have traditionally been aimed at women, but men are spending more and more money on hair care, too. Products that claim to reduce baldness are doing particularly well (see page 40).

HAIR COLOURANTS

What are ombré and balayage? They are different ways of lightening your hair. The ombré look is having highlights that start halfway down the hair and get paler towards the tips. Balayage is the painting of streaks onto hair.

Stars such as Katy Perry have set trends for blue, red and pink hair.

Out of the salon

More and more people are colouring their hair at home, and cosmetics companies bring out new products all the time to meet the demand. In the United Kingdom, each woman spends around £230 a year on hair colouring, part of an annual business worth well over £300 million.

The lighter red streaks in this model's hair have been painted on with a brush. This technique is called balayage.

FUTURE FACT

Hair colourants are very popular and people are becoming more and more adventurous. Recently, celebrities have been adding grey to their hair! They bleach their hair silver white, or add silver or grey streaks or tips.

Covering up grey

Grey hair is associated with growing old, so it is not surprising that many people with grey hair want to change their hair colour. Many women, and an increasing number of men, will add blonde or darker dyes to their hair to hide the grey.

STRAIGHT OR CURLY?

Who spends most on haircare? According to Treasured Locks, a company that sells haircare products, African-American women spend between double and six times what other Americans spend on haircare. One of the most common treatments they buy is hair relaxing, which softens and straightens the hair.

Hair relaxers

Hair relaxers use strong chemicals to soften and relax the hair. The strongest ones can easily damage the hair and scalp. Hair relaxing and straightening should be done only by an expert in a salon.

A black person's hair is often naturally curly. To achieve a straight style, strong chemicals must be used to relax the hair.

The trend for long hair has led to an increase in demand for coloured hair extensions.

Hair extensions

Why waste time growing your hair when you can buy hair extensions to attach to your own hair? That is what many women think and the market in hair extensions is growing. Extensions make a lot of money for the hair salons, which can charge up to £800 for a full extension treatment.

UNWANTED HAIR

Some people have more hair than they want! Hair grows all over the body except on the lips, palms of the hands and on the soles of the feet. Body hair has become increasingly unfashionable for men as well as for women and the beauty industry has risen to the challenge.

Creams and waxes

Shaving is the easiest way to get rid of hair, but the hair soon grows back. Creams and waxes remove hair for longer and leave skin smoother. While shaving cuts the hair at the surface of the skin, creams dissolve it and waxes pull it out at the roots.

During waxing, the skin is covered with wax. Then a paper strip is laid over the wax and quickly removed, pulling off both the wax and the hair.

FUTURE FACT

Laser hair removal is expected to grow, making more money for salons and manufacturers. In 2010, sales of laser devices reached £640 million worldwide, and by 2017 they are expected to reach £1.4 billion.

Plucking eyebrows can be difficult to do well. Many women choose to have their eyebrows professionally shaped in a salon instead.

Electrolysis and hair removal

Electrolysis uses electricity to kill the hair root and so remove hairs one by one. Lasers, which use a beam of light to do much the same thing, are taking over this market, as larger areas can be treated more quickly.

SHAVING

When did shaving become big business? Sales of Gillette's safety razor with disposable blades boomed after every soldier fighting in the United States' army was supplied with one during the First World War. Today, companies compete to produce better razors, blades, shaving creams and shaving lotions.

Razor sharp

Electric razors were invented in 1928, but safety razors continued to be popular. Many men prefer to use a traditional razor with water and shaving foam or gel. Companies selling shaving products to men often use the language of fast cars and jet planes for their products, such as Gillette's Mach 3 Turbo razor.

Most men shave every day. Shaving is big business for companies selling razors and shaving foam.

Shaving foams, creams and lotions

Companies are constantly developing new or better shaving products, such as gels that irritate the skin less, pre-shaving lotions and aftershaves. The biggest companies are those that produce razors, such as Gillette, and those that make other skincare products.

Razors are made for women, too. Women use them to shave their legs and under their arms.

FUTURE FACT

In 2014, Europe saw more than £70 million wiped off sales of shaving products. The main cause was a new trend for men to grow beards. Sales are likely to rise, though, when the fashion changes again to a clean-shaven look.

CHAPTER 4

UNDER THE KNIFE

Why is cosmetic surgery so expensive? Cosmetic surgery is done to change a person's looks, not to improve their health. This means that the operations are not necessary and so are not usually covered by health services. The cosmetic surgery business is growing rapidly. It is worth more than £3 billion pounds a year in the United Kingdom and $1 million in Australia.

Many women do not like the face they see when they look in the mirror. Other people, though, can see nothing wrong with it!

Common operations

The most popular operation is changing the size or shape of the breasts. This is done by implanting a silicone rubber shell filled with silicone gel or salt water. Liposuction is also popular. In this operation, fat is sucked out of selected areas, such as the thighs, hips or tummy.

FIGHTING FAT

Only small amounts of fat can be removed by liposuction. It is not a solution for the growing problem of obesity. The only way to lose weight overall is to eat a healthy diet and to exercise regularly.

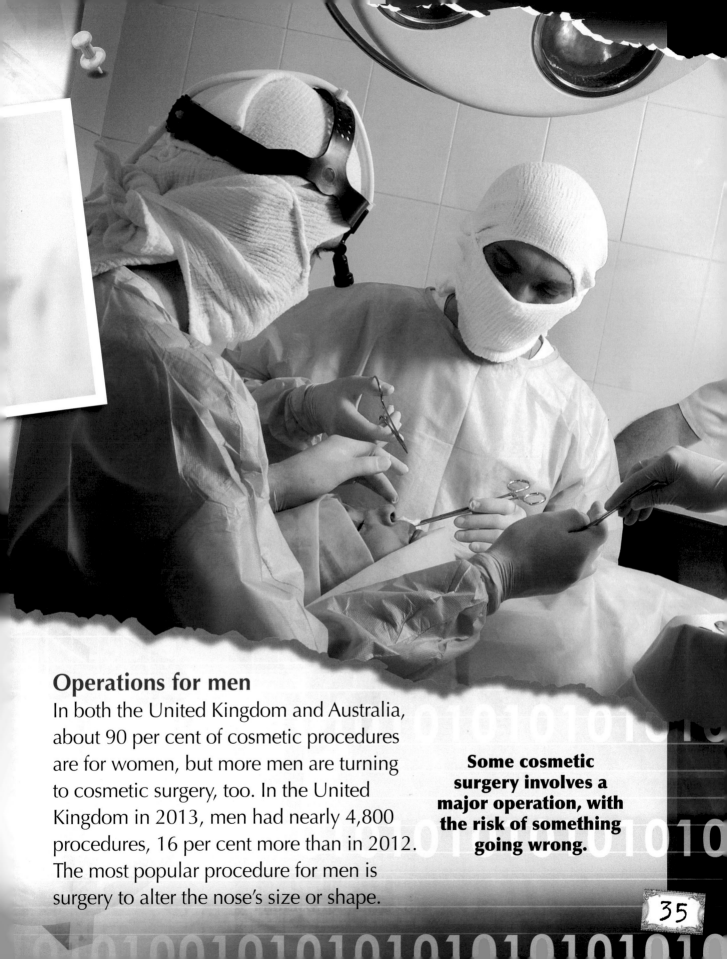

Operations for men

In both the United Kingdom and Australia, about 90 per cent of cosmetic procedures are for women, but more men are turning to cosmetic surgery, too. In the United Kingdom in 2013, men had nearly 4,800 procedures, 16 per cent more than in 2012. The most popular procedure for men is surgery to alter the nose's size or shape.

Some cosmetic surgery involves a major operation, with the risk of something going wrong.

IMPROVING ON NATURE

Many people wish they could change something about their body. More and more people spend a lot of money to make that wish come true. Why are people so dissatisfied with the way they look? Some women want to be more like the celebrities they see in films or on television. Others think they should look like models on posters or in magazines.

Celebrities such as Jennifer Lopez are often suspected of having had cosmetic surgery, whether they have or not.

Media images

Most models and some film stars rely on their looks to earn their living. They spend a lot of time and money to look the way they do. Often they have cosmetic surgery – the most expensive and extreme way of changing a person's appearance.

Many women would love to have a slim figure like this model. Some women are even prepared to have cosmetic surgery to get it!

FUTURE FACT

Americans spend more on cosmetic surgery than anyone else. In 2013, they spent an incredible £4 billion on surgical procedures – 11 per cent more than the year before. The figures are likely to grow in the years to come.

Young and slim

Models are almost always young and extremely slim. Many women feel a failure if they do not match up to the impossible standard of celebrities and models. Youthful looks are the most admired, which means that most older women try to look younger than they are.

FOREVER YOUNG

Why do women try to look younger?

Most women say that looking younger makes them feel good and more confident. In the past, some women older than 50 or 60 had a facelift, which is a surgical operation. Today, women as young as 20 are using cheaper ways to enhance their looks, creating a business worth nearly £2 billion in the United Kingdom alone.

Botox is injected under the skin, mainly to get rid of fine wrinkles. Its effect lasts only about three months.

Botox bonanza

An injection of Botulinum toxin, or Botox, is the most popular non-surgical cosmetic procedure in the world. In 2013, more than 5 million treatments were given worldwide – for men as well as women. Even some dentists offer Botox injections.

In the past, older women used anti-ageing creams to reduce wrinkles and make their skin look younger. Now, even young women feel under pressure to use them.

TOO MUCH BOTOX

A small amount of Botox injected into a muscle makes it relax. In large quantities, however, Botox is a dangerous poison. When too much is used, or it is used too often, a person's face looks frozen and he or she cannot smile properly.

The business of staying young

Botox, creams and other anti-ageing treatments are big business. Companies charge more for anti-ageing products than for regular cosmetics and the market is likely to increase. By 2019, the global anti-ageing business is expected to be worth more than £120 billion.

A FULL HEAD OF HAIR

Is there a cure for baldness? Many men and the haircare business wish there was! Baldness can be treated but not cured. The first company to find a cure will make a fortune. To date, the best treatments for baldness include Regaine foam and Propecia tablets, as well as hair implants.

Hair restorers

About one-fifth of 20-year-old white males are already losing some hair. By the age of 50, about half of this group are beginning to go bald. Regaine and Propecia each contain a drug that slows the process down and encourages new hair to grow. As soon as the man stops taking the drug, however, the baldness simply returns.

Many men are happy being bald. Some even choose it, by shaving their heads.

This man is checking to see if his hair is getting thinner, which is an early sign of balding.

FUTURE FACT

The global market for Regaine and Propecia is increasing by almost 5 per cent a year. In 2010, it was worth almost £1.2 billion. By 2017, it is expected to reach £1.6 billion, an increase of £400 million.

Hair implants

Some men resort to hair implants. Hair from the back of the head is moved and implanted into the bare patches. To get a natural-looking result, many hairs have to be implanted. The procedure can cost up to £7,000 and does not work for everyone.

THE PERFECT SMILE

Do perfect teeth make a perfect smile? Cosmetic dentists have persuaded most of us that the answer is 'yes'. Improving the appearance and colour of teeth is big business. Many children (and some adults) have a brace fitted to straighten crooked teeth. The cost for these treatments can add up to thousands of pounds.

Most braces are made of metal. Ceramic or see-through braces are invisible, but more expensive.

Even and straight

Straight teeth not only improve a person's smile but are also easier to clean and this helps to keep the teeth and gums healthy. Some braces are designed to change the position of the lower jaw, so that the person's 'bite' is improved.

BUYING OVERSEAS

Some cosmetic dentistry is so expensive that many people go abroad for treatment. Prices in Hungary, Cyprus and India are cheaper, for example, than in the United Kingdom or Australia. If a problem arises after the treatment, however, it can be difficult to get it fixed.

Straight, white teeth are a sign of good health – but it can cost a lot to achieve the look.

Whiter and brighter

Toothpaste that contains whitener is cheap, but it can only do so much. Veneers and lumineers are special surfaces that are fixed over the teeth. They cost up to £1,500 a tooth. Even more expensive are tooth implants, which are fixed into the jawbone.

CHALLENGES AHEAD

Does the future look bright for beauty companies? Business forecasters predict that sales in most areas of the beauty industry will grow over the next five years, but are they right? Those forecasts assume that people will have more money to spend. When times are bad, though, people have less money and most businesses sell less. The beauty industry, however, may be different.

Many cosmetic giants, such as Chanel, use high-profile stars like Nicole Kidman to advertise their products.

Appearance matters

When businesses are doing badly, people worry about losing their job or finding a new one. Instead of spending less on cosmetics, many people spend more. They want to look their best to impress employers or simply to feel better about themselves in difficult times.

Celebrity beauty products are a growing trend. Many stars, such as Kim Kardashian, are launching their own cosmetic brands.

FUTURE FACT

Looking and feeling beautiful has been linked to good health. The beauty industry has responded quickly to this by producing more natural and organic brands of cosmetics and haircare. What else may follow?

New trends and products

The beauty industry continues to develop new and better products. Clinique makes cosmetics for people with sensitive skins, who may suffer from allergies. Its products are expensive, but it has become one of Estée Lauder's most successful brands.

GLOSSARY

animal testing testing a product on an animal. Companies can use only ingredients that have been tested on animals or people, but the tests often cause the animals to suffer.

aromatherapy a treatment based on the external use of aromatic plant oils to maintain and promote good health

beauty products creams, lotions, make-up and nail and hair products that people use to improve and take care of their appearance

beauty therapist a person who has been trained to give beauty treatments, such as manicures

cosmetic surgery an operation performed to improve the way a person looks

cosmetics products that people use to care for their skin or hair and to make themselves look better

economists people who study how goods, services and wealth are produced, sold and bought

electrolysis a way of removing hair roots by using an electric current

facelift cosmetic surgery that lifts the skin on the face to remove wrinkles and sagging flesh

facial beauty treatment for the face that may include massage, cleansing the skin and applying make-up

hair relaxer a lotion or cream that contains strong chemicals, which make curly hair straighter and softer

implant something that is inserted into parts of the body, using surgery

kohl black powder that contains some metals. It is traditionally used as eyeliner, applied with a kohl pencil

laser a strong, narrow beam of light

manicurist a person who trims, cleans and polishes someone else's nails

massage rubbing the skin and muscles

meditation a form of relaxation that calms and focuses the mind

moisturising making something, such as skin, less dry by applying creams

radiation energy in the form of rays

research actions taken to find out new information about a particular subject

safety razor a razor in which the blade is mostly covered

silicone a type of synthetic material that feels like rubber

skincare cosmetics or actions for taking care of the skin

smallpox a serious disease that can leave permanent marks on the skin

spa a luxurious hotel or other place where different types of beauty treatments, such as massages and facials, are available

sunscreen a cream or lotion that protects skin from being damaged by the sun's rays

FOR MORE INFORMATION

BOOKS

Estée Lauder (Essential Lives), Robert Grayson, Essential Library

The Faces Behind Beauty (Business Leaders), Wanda Langley, Morgan Reynolds Publishing

Cosmetic Surgery (Ethical Debates), Kaye Stearman, Wayland

WEBSITES

Find out more about the beauty industry at:

www.chemistscorner.com/how-to-become-a-cosmetic-chemist

www.cosmeticsinfo.org/history3.php

www.loreal.com

Note to parents and teachers
Every effort has been made by the Publisher to ensure that these websites contain no inappropriate or offensive material. However, because of the nature of the Internet, it is impossible to guarantee that the contents of these sites will not be altered. We strongly advise that Internet access is supervised by a responsible adult.

INDEX

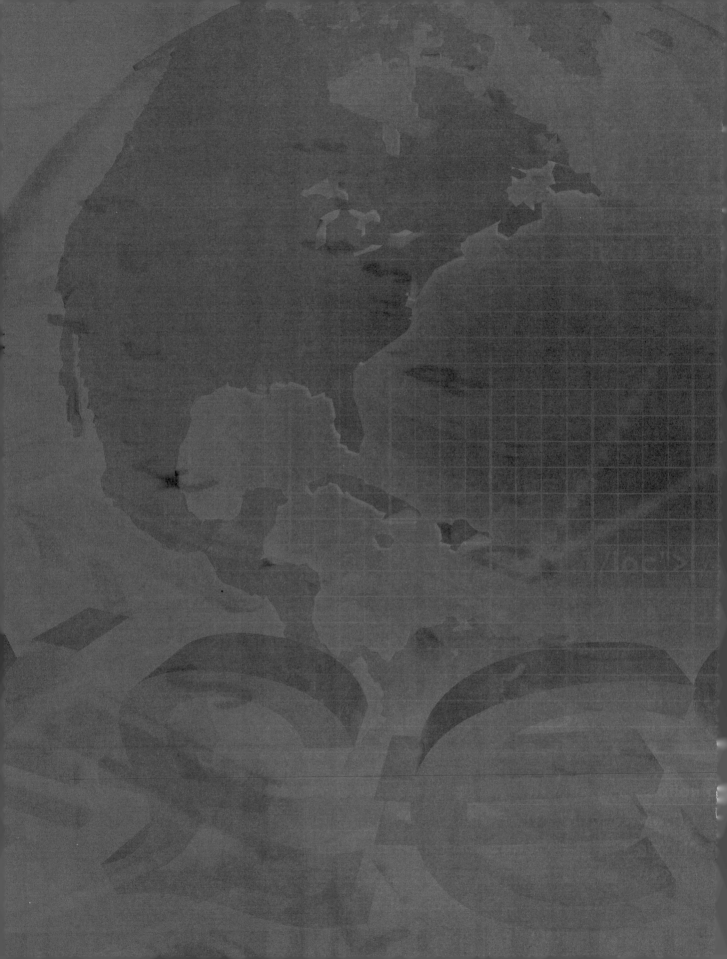